Graduation Guest book

In Celebration of

_____

_____

_____

Class of _____

Graduation Photo

Graduation Photo

School Highlights

My plans for the future

Guest _____

Memories _____

_____

_____

_____

Life Advice _____

_____

_____

_____

Wishes _____

_____

_____

_____

Guest _____

Memories _____

_____

_____

_____

Life Advice _____

_____

_____

Wishes _____

_____

_____

_____

Guest _____

Memories _____

_____

_____

_____

Life Advice _____

_____

_____

_____

Wishes _____

_____

_____

_____

Guest _____

Memories _____

_____

_____

_____

Life Advice _____

_____

_____

_____

Wishes _____

_____

_____

_____

Guest _____

Memories _____
_____
_____
_____

Life Advice _____
_____
_____
_____

Wishes _____
_____
_____
_____

Guest _____

Memories _____

_____

_____

_____

Life Advice _____

_____

_____

_____

Wishes _____

_____

_____

_____

Guest _____

Memories _____

_____

_____

_____

Life Advice _____

_____

_____

_____

Wishes _____

_____

_____

_____

Guest _____

Memories _____

_____

_____

Life Advice _____

_____

_____

Wishes _____

_____

_____

Guest _____

Memories _____

_____

_____

Life Advice _____

_____

_____

_____

Wishes _____

_____

_____

_____

Guest _____

Memories _____

_____

_____

_____

Life Advice _____

_____

_____

_____

Wishes _____

_____

_____

_____

Guest _____

Memories _____

_____

_____

Life Advice _____

_____

_____

Wishes _____

_____

_____

Guest _____

Memories _____

_____

_____

_____

Life Advice _____

_____

_____

Wishes _____

_____

_____

_____

Guest _____

Memories _____

_____

_____

_____

Life Advice _____

_____

_____

Wishes _____

_____

_____

_____

Guest _____

Memories _____

_____

_____

_____

Life Advice _____

_____

_____

_____

Wishes _____

_____

_____

_____

Guest _____

Memories _____

_____

_____

_____

Life Advice _____

_____

_____

_____

Wishes _____

_____

_____

_____

Guest _____

Memories _____

_____

_____

Life Advice _____

_____

_____

Wishes _____

_____

_____

Guest _____

Memories _____

_____

_____

Life Advice _____

_____

_____

Wishes _____

_____

_____

Guest _____

Memories _____

_____

_____

_____

Life Advice _____

_____

_____

_____

Wishes _____

_____

_____

_____

Guest _____

Memories _____

_____

_____

_____

Life Advice _____

_____

_____

_____

Wishes _____

_____

_____

_____

Guest _____

Memories _____

_____

_____

_____

Life Advice _____

_____

_____

Wishes _____

_____

_____

Guest _____

Memories _____

_____

_____

_____

Life Advice _____

_____

_____

_____

Wishes _____

_____

_____

_____

Guest _____

Memories _____

_____

_____

_____

Life Advice _____

_____

_____

_____

Wishes _____

_____

_____

_____

Guest _____

Memories _____

_____

_____

_____

Life Advice _____

_____

_____

_____

Wishes _____

_____

_____

Guest _____

Memories _____
_____
_____
_____

Life Advice _____
_____
_____
_____

Wishes _____
_____
_____
_____

Guest _____

Memories _____

_____

_____

_____

Life Advice _____

_____

_____

_____

Wishes _____

_____

_____

_____

Guest _____

Memories _____

_____

_____

_____

Life Advice _____

_____

_____

_____

Wishes _____

_____

_____

_____

$Guest$ _____

$Memories$ _____

_____

_____

_____

$Life\ Advice$ _____

_____

_____

_____

$Wishes$ _____

_____

_____

_____

Guest _____

Memories _____

_____

_____

_____

Life Advice _____

_____

_____

_____

Wishes _____

_____

_____

_____

Guest _____

Memories _____

_____

_____

_____

Life Advice _____

_____

_____

_____

Wishes _____

_____

_____

_____

Guest _____

Memories _____

_____

_____

_____

Life Advice _____

_____

_____

_____

Wishes _____

_____

_____

_____

Guest _____

Memories _____

_____

_____

Life Advice _____

_____

_____

_____

Wishes _____

_____

_____

_____

Guest _____

Memories _____

_____

_____

_____

Life Advice _____

_____

_____

Wishes _____

_____

_____

Guest _____

Memories _____

_____

_____

_____

Life Advice _____

_____

_____

_____

Wishes _____

_____

_____

_____

Guest _____

Memories _____

_____

_____

_____

Life Advice _____

_____

_____

_____

Wishes _____

_____

_____

_____

Guest _____

Memories _____

_____

_____

_____

Life Advice _____

_____

_____

_____

Wishes _____

_____

_____

_____

Guest _____

Memories _____

_____

_____

_____

Life Advice _____

_____

_____

_____

Wishes _____

_____

_____

_____

Guest _____

Memories _____

_____

_____

_____

Life Advice _____

_____

_____

_____

Wishes _____

_____

_____

_____

Guest _____

Memories _____

_____

_____

_____

Life Advice _____

_____

_____

Wishes _____

_____

_____

_____

Guest _____

Memories _____

_____

_____

_____

Life Advice _____

_____

_____

_____

Wishes _____

_____

_____

_____

Guest _____

Memories _____

_____

_____

_____

Life Advice _____

_____

_____

_____

Wishes _____

_____

_____

_____

Guest _____

Memories _____

_____

_____

_____

Life Advice _____

_____

_____

_____

Wishes _____

_____

_____

_____

Guest _____

Memories _____

_____

_____

_____

Life Advice _____

_____

_____

Wishes _____

_____

_____

Guest _____

Memories _____

_____

_____

_____

Life Advice _____

_____

_____

_____

Wishes _____

_____

_____

Guest _____

Memories _____

_____

_____

_____

Life Advice _____

_____

_____

_____

Wishes _____

_____

_____

_____

Guest _____

Memories _____

_____

_____

_____

Life Advice _____

_____

_____

_____

Wishes _____

_____

_____

_____

Guest _____

Memories _____

_____

_____

_____

Life Advice _____

_____

_____

_____

Wishes _____

_____

_____

_____

Guest _____

Memories _____

_____

_____

_____

Life Advice _____

_____

_____

_____

Wishes _____

_____

_____

_____

Guest _____

Memories _____

_____

_____

_____

Life Advice _____

_____

_____

Wishes _____

_____

_____

Guest _____

Memories _____

_____

_____

Life Advice _____

_____

_____

Wishes _____

_____

_____

_____

Guest _____

Memories _____
_____
_____
_____

Life Advice _____
_____
_____

Wishes _____
_____
_____
_____

Guest _____

Memories _____

_____

_____

_____

Life Advice _____

_____

_____

_____

Wishes _____

_____

_____

_____

Guest _____

Memories _____
_____
_____
_____

Life Advice _____
_____
_____
_____

Wishes _____
_____
_____
_____

Guest _____

Memories _____

_____

_____

_____

Life Advice _____

_____

_____

_____

Wishes _____

_____

_____

_____

Guest _____

Memories _____

_____

_____

_____

Life Advice _____

_____

_____

Wishes _____

_____

_____

Guest _____

Memories _____

_____

_____

_____

Life Advice _____

_____

_____

_____

Wishes _____

_____

_____

_____

Guest _____

Memories _____

_____

_____

_____

Life Advice _____

_____

_____

_____

Wishes _____

_____

_____

_____

Guest _____

Memories _____

_____

_____

Life Advice _____

_____

_____

_____

Wishes _____

_____

_____

_____

Guest _____

Memories _____

_____

_____

_____

Life Advice _____

_____

_____

_____

Wishes _____

_____

_____

_____

Guest _____

Memories _____
_____
_____
_____

Life Advice _____
_____
_____
_____

Wishes _____
_____
_____
_____

Guest _____

Memories _____
_____
_____
_____

Life Advice _____
_____
_____
_____

Wishes _____
_____
_____
_____

Guest _____

Memories _____

_____

_____

_____

Life Advice _____

_____

_____

_____

Wishes _____

_____

_____

_____

Guest _____

Memories _____

_____

_____

_____

Life Advice _____

_____

_____

_____

Wishes _____

_____

_____

_____

Guest _____

Memories _____

_____

_____

_____

Life Advice _____

_____

_____

_____

Wishes _____

_____

_____

_____

Guest _____

Memories _____

_____

_____

_____

Life Advice _____

_____

_____

_____

Wishes _____

_____

_____

_____

Guest _____

Memories _____

_____

_____

_____

Life Advice _____

_____

_____

_____

Wishes _____

_____

_____

_____

Guest _____

Memories _____

_____

_____

_____

Life Advice _____

_____

_____

_____

Wishes _____

_____

_____

_____

Guest _____

Memories _____

_____

_____

_____

Life Advice _____

_____

_____

_____

Wishes _____

_____

_____

_____

Guest _____

Memories _____

_____

_____

_____

Life Advice _____

_____

_____

_____

Wishes _____

_____

_____

_____

Guest _____

Memories _____

_____

_____

_____

Life Advice _____

_____

_____

_____

Wishes _____

_____

_____

_____

Guest _____

Memories _____

_____

_____

_____

Life Advice _____

_____

_____

_____

Wishes _____

_____

_____

_____

Guest _____

Memories _____

_____

_____

_____

Life Advice _____

_____

_____

_____

Wishes _____

_____

_____

_____

Guest _____

Memories _____

_____

_____

_____

Life Advice _____

_____

_____

_____

Wishes _____

_____

_____

_____

Guest _____

Memories _____

_____

_____

_____

Life Advice _____

_____

_____

_____

Wishes _____

_____

_____

_____

Guest _____

Memories _____

_____

_____

_____

Life Advice _____

_____

_____

_____

Wishes _____

_____

_____

_____

Guest _____

Memories _____

_____

_____

_____

Life Advice _____

_____

_____

_____

Wishes _____

_____

_____

_____

Guest _____

Memories _____

_____

_____

_____

Life Advice _____

_____

_____

_____

Wishes _____

_____

_____

_____

Guest _____

Memories _____

_____

_____

_____

Life Advice _____

_____

_____

_____

Wishes _____

_____

_____

_____

Guest _____

Memories _____
_____
_____
_____

Life Advice _____
_____
_____
_____

Wishes _____
_____
_____
_____

Guest _____

Memories _____

_____

_____

Life Advice _____

_____

_____

Wishes _____

_____

_____

_____

Guest _____

Memories _____

_____

_____

_____

Life Advice _____

_____

_____

_____

Wishes _____

_____

_____

_____

Guest _____

Memories _____

_____

_____

_____

Life Advice _____

_____

_____

Wishes _____

_____

_____

Guest _____

Memories _____

_____

_____

_____

Life Advice _____

_____

_____

Wishes _____

_____

_____

Guest _____

Memories _____

_____

_____

_____

Life Advice _____

_____

_____

_____

Wishes _____

_____

_____

_____

Guest _____

Memories _____

_____

_____

_____

Life Advice _____

_____

_____

_____

Wishes _____

_____

_____

_____

Guest _____

Memories _____

_____

_____

Life Advice _____

_____

_____

Wishes _____

_____

_____

Guest _____

Memories _____

_____

_____

_____

Life Advice _____

_____

_____

_____

Wishes _____

_____

_____

_____

Guest _____

Memories _____

_____

_____

_____

Life Advice _____

_____

_____

_____

Wishes _____

_____

_____

_____

Guest _____

Memories _____

_____

_____

_____

Life Advice _____

_____

_____

_____

Wishes _____

_____

_____

_____

Guest _____

Memories _____

_____

_____

_____

Life Advice _____

_____

_____

_____

Wishes _____

_____

_____

_____

Guest _____

Memories _____

_____

_____

_____

Life Advice _____

_____

_____

_____

Wishes _____

_____

_____

_____

Guest _____

Memories _____

_____

_____

_____

Life Advice _____

_____

_____

_____

Wishes _____

_____

_____

_____

Guest _____

Memories _____

_____

_____

_____

Life Advice _____

_____

_____

Wishes _____

_____

_____

Guest _____

Memories _____

_____

_____

_____

Life Advice _____

_____

_____

_____

Wishes _____

_____

_____

_____

Guest _____

Memories _____
_____
_____
_____

Life Advice _____
_____
_____
_____

Wishes _____
_____
_____
_____

$Guest$ _____

$Memories$ _____

_____

_____

_____

$Life\ Advice$ _____

_____

_____

_____

$Wishes$ _____

_____

_____

_____

Guest _____

Memories _____

_____

_____

_____

Life Advice _____

_____

_____

Wishes _____

_____

_____

Guest _____

Memories _____

_____

_____

_____

Life Advice _____

_____

_____

_____

Wishes _____

_____

_____

_____

Guest _____

Memories _____

_____

_____

Life Advice _____

_____

_____

Wishes _____

_____

_____

Guest _____

Memories _____

_____

_____

_____

Life Advice _____

_____

_____

_____

Wishes _____

_____

_____

_____

Guest _____

Memories _____

_____

_____

_____

Life Advice _____

_____

_____

Wishes _____

_____

_____

_____

Guest _____

Memories _____

_____

_____

Life Advice _____

_____

_____

Wishes _____

_____

_____

_____

Guest _____

Memories _____

_____

_____

_____

Life Advice _____

_____

_____

Wishes _____

_____

_____

_____

Guest _____

Memories _____

_____

_____

_____

Life Advice _____

_____

_____

Wishes _____

_____

_____

_____

Guest _____

Memories _____
_____
_____
_____

Life Advice _____
_____
_____
_____

Wishes _____
_____
_____
_____

Guest _____

Memories _____

_____

_____

_____

Life Advice _____

_____

_____

_____

Wishes _____

_____

_____

_____

Guest _____

Memories _____
_____
_____

Life Advice _____
_____
_____

Wishes _____
_____
_____

Guest _____

Memories _____

_____

_____

_____

Life Advice _____

_____

_____

_____

Wishes _____

_____

_____

_____

Guest _____

Memories _____

_____

_____

_____

Life Advice _____

_____

_____

_____

Wishes _____

_____

_____

_____

Guest _____

Memories _____

_____

_____

Life Advice _____

_____

_____

Wishes _____

_____

_____

Guest _____

Memories _____

_____

_____

_____

Life Advice _____

_____

_____

_____

Wishes _____

_____

_____

_____

Guest _____

Memories _____

_____

_____

Life Advice _____

_____

_____

Wishes _____

_____

_____

Guest _____

Memories _____
_____
_____
_____

Life Advice _____
_____
_____
_____

Wishes _____
_____
_____
_____

Guest _____

Memories _____

_____

_____

_____

Life Advice _____

_____

_____

Wishes _____

_____

_____

_____

Guest _____

Memories _____

_____

_____

Life Advice _____

_____

_____

Wishes _____

_____

_____

Guest _____

Memories _____

_____

_____

_____

Life Advice _____

_____

_____

_____

Wishes _____

_____

_____

_____

Made in the USA
Monee, IL
06 June 2022

97553458R00068